THE CUDDLE SUTRA

An Unabashed Celebration of the Ultimate Intimacy

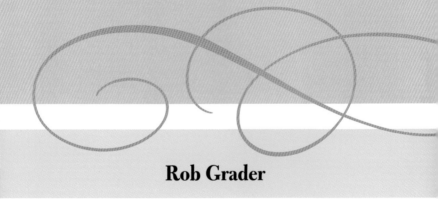

Rob Grader

sourcebooks
casablanca

Published by Sourcebooks Casablanca, an imprint of Sourcebooks, Inc.
P.O. Box 4410, Naperville, Illinois 60567–4410
(630) 961–3900
FAX: (630) 961–2168

www.sourcebooks.com

Printed and bound in China
OGP 10 9 8 7 6 5 4 3

Karen,
Come cuddle with me.

ACKNOWLEDGMENTS

As impossible as it is to cuddle by yourself, try writing a book alone. It just cannot be done. Here are the very special and wonderful people who have embraced the idea of the *Cuddle Sutra* and helped me create it: First and foremost to my wife Karen, words are not enough to express my gratitude not only for being my constant cuddling companion, but truly the inspiration and co-creator of this book (not to mention a heck of a good proofreader). I will cuddle with you now and always. And to my newest cuddling partner, my baby boy Roscoe, you have brought new dimensions to my life and to my cuddling. I am also grateful for the encouragement and assistance of Ken Bolden, Steve Harper, Paul Dinas, Deb Werksman, Rebecca Kilbreath, Megan Dempster and everyone at Sourcebooks. Additionally, there is a long list of friends and family members who are always willing to listen to and support my kooky ideas: my family, including Mom, Dad, Jeff, Lisa, Emily, Sally, Jonas, Stu, Ellen, Jessica, Michelle, Scott, Trish, Lulu, Elaine, Maxine, Gary, Joe, and Marybeth; and my extended family of friends: Billy, Bill, Sue, Mark, Danny, Suzi, Chiori, Shari, Bob, Patricia, Janice, Michael, Helen, as well as all my friends at Bliss Spa and Madison Plaza.

I offer you all my deepest thanks and tightest hugs!

TABLE OF CONTENTS

We spend about a third of our lives in bed, giving us time to explore the many varieties of bedroom cuddling positions that range from traditional to the seemingly acrobatic.

Chapter 2: Couch Canoodling: Snuggling on the Sofa   47

Whether watching TV, having a heart-to-heart discussion, or reading the Sunday paper, these positions take multitasking to a whole new level.

Part Two: Public Displays of Affection

While you may not think of holding hands and public embraces as cuddling, they are indeed the purest and most common forms of the cuddle. Do not be fooled by their simplicity—these are powerfully emotional acts. You may be surprised at the infinite number of ways two people can manage to walk and be in love at the same time.

INTRODUCTION

*"Despite what you've been told, men love to cuddle . . .
but why does your head have to block the TV?"*
—DENNIS MILLER

It all started, not surprisingly, in bed one Saturday morning. The second Saturday in October to be precise. My wife and I have a tendency to overbook our weekend schedules, but this was one of those rare days when we did not need to jump out of bed at the crack of dawn to meet someone before we had to get somewhere to do something. Our slate was wide open. Sure, the shopping needed to be done, the laundry was piling up, and the bathroom needed a serious scrubbing, but the chores were nothing that couldn't be put off. It was that precious day when we could indulge ourselves in a serious little cuddling session.

Now, when I say we had some time for cuddling, that is not some prudish allusion to sex. I mean the pure thing—cuddling, snuggling, canoodling, billing and cooing, and yes, maybe even a little petting, caressing, and tickling for good measure. Now don't get me wrong, there is nothing wrong with sex. Sex is a great thing but cuddling is the ultimate intimate act; more than a candlelit dinner, more than a joint tax return, and yes, even more than sex. It is an act of pure physical communication; it's how we express our affection, our connection, devotion, vulnerability, and generosity. Within the simple act of an embrace, two people can be joined together in such an intense bond that words no longer serve a purpose. The cuddle says it all.

Let's face it, we can have sex with someone without it meaning much, but it is pretty close to impossible to enjoy some casual cuddling. In fact, it may well be the best test of whether or not that person in your bed is the right one for you. Try it out. Hold him tight and close, wrap your arms around her, intermingle your legs, stroke his hair. Now do a quick gut check. Does this feel right? Do you want this to go on and on? Or are you counting the seconds until you can get out of bed without seeming harsh? When you are this physically intimate with someone, your instincts will always tell you the truth.

Cuddling is one of the great pleasures of life and it is also one of the most basic human needs. Plainly stated, human beings simply cannot survive without the touch of another person. Clinical studies at The Touch Institute at The University of Miami and other institutions have shown that infants who go without being held and touched show developmental delays in areas from weight gain to cognitive and motor skills. These studies have also shown that throughout our lives, the touch of another can have a dramatic effect on such conditions as depression, arthritis, asthma, ADHD, autism, diabetes, fibromyalgia, hypertension, and migraine headaches.

The human being was built to experience touch. Starting with our skin and extending into every layer of the body, touch is a sense that is fully incorporated into all facets of our lives. The effects of touch go beyond our physical experience and even have a proven impact on the chemistry of our emotional life. Studies have shown that massage and other forms of touch increase the feel-good chemicals serotonin and dopamine in the brain—the exact effect people strive for by taking antidepressants.

But I didn't set out to write a scientific tract on cuddling; this is a celebration of the cuddle. It is an all-encompassing resource for the act of cuddling. The book is filled with detailed descriptions and illustrations of the ways to express affection for one another whether in the privacy of your own bedroom or walking down Main Street. It is an affectionate look at coupling that is both exhilarating and welcoming to all. The perfect resource for sharing love that is literally no holds barred.

Back to that lazy October day, the second Saturday in October. Remember? There we were, cuddling and snuggling. "We should get up." "Yeah, we should." And embracing and hugging. "You want to take a walk?" "Yeah . . . in a little while." And nuzzling and petting. "Do you want to grab some lunch?" "Yeah, I guess we should . . ." By now the cuddle-fest had migrated to the couch. " . . . or do you just want to spend the rest of the day cuddling?" "Yeaaah!" And so it was that our own personal holiday was born. The second Saturday in October is now and shall forever be National Cuddle Day. We never left the house that day, and we never had a more perfect day together . . . until, of course, the next Cuddle Day rolled around.

The Three T's of Cuddling

There is no wrong way to cuddle, but there are ways to make your cuddles more intimate and enjoyable. Here are the three T's of cuddling to keep in mind, which can be applied to almost any cuddling position in the book.

TALK—once you are physically communicating with your partner through the cuddle, verbal communication will have even more of an impact. From goofy pillow talk to those quiet monumental conversations about hopes, dreams, and wishes, share what you are thinking and feeling—the impact of your cuddles will be even more intense.

TOUCH—While your bodies may be tied up in knots around each other in some of these positions, your hands always have at least some range of motion to touch your partner. There are at least four basic types of touch that work particularly well with cuddles:

caressing, tickling, scratching, and light fingertip touch—use them all!

TOGETHERNESS—Gravity is a remarkable tool for cuddling, and one that should never be shied away from. In whatever position you find yourselves, take advantage of any opportunity to let the full weight of your body rest effortlessly on your partner. Whether it is your whole body or just an arm or leg, allow the full heft of your bodies to make the cuddle more comforting and substantial.

A Note about the Positions and the Descriptions

One of the magical things about cuddling is that anyone can do it. It is not limited by gender, age, size, or acrobatic abilities. One of the not so magical things about writing a book is that in order to be clear and understandable, you are forced to use pronouns like he and she. For the sake of clarity, I have described each cuddle with genders to correspond with the accompanying illustration. In reality, just about every role in every cuddle in this book can be performed by any partner in any relationship.

Depending on you and your partner's size and body types, you may find there are a few positions in the book that are not a perfect fit for you. In these rare cases, I would encourage you to experiment and communicate. Shift a leg here, an arm there, roll a bit more to the side—whatever it might take for you to be comfortable and at ease in that position. Above all else, a cuddle must be comfortable for it to be comforting.

"We are, each of us, angels with only one wing,
and we can only fly embracing each other."

—LUCIANO DECRESCENZO

PART ONE

Private Displays
of Affection

CHAPTER 1

Bedroom Boogie: Cuddling in Bed

COME TO PAPA

This is the classic, all-purpose, stay-snuggled-up-close-to-me-all-night-long cuddle. He is lying on his back, she is lying on her side completely resting all of her weight against him. He gently hugs her upper body with his arm, supporting her neck and head. She hugs him with her upper arm and tucks her lower arm into her chest so it rests between their two bodies. She may feel the urge to slide this arm under his body to give him a complete hug, but if you maintain that position for too long, her arm will eventually go numb from the weight of his body, and it is not particularly comfortable for him. You will find your legs intermingling; let them rest wherever is most comfortable. This position is all about maximum contact and maximum comfort. This one also works like a dream on the couch.

68½

It's not what you think . . . well it is, but not in the way you think. You are both lying on your side facing each other, head to toe. Your knees are slightly bent with the bottom knee lying slightly forward of the other knee, leaving your inner thigh to form a perfect pillow for your partner's head. This is a surprisingly intimate position that is ideal for light caressing and sensual tickling on the lower back, behind, and thighs.

LAP OF LUXURY

This is the perfect pick-me-up cuddle. If one of you is down in the dumps, stressed out, or just needs a little TLC, this will make everything right with the world once more. She sits cross-legged on the bed with her legs making a cradle for his head. He lies on his side with his head nestled in her lap and the rest of his body is wrapped around her body in a kind of fetal position. This will leave his back available for the back scratch of his dreams while being a very easy position for both of you to maintain for an extended length of time.

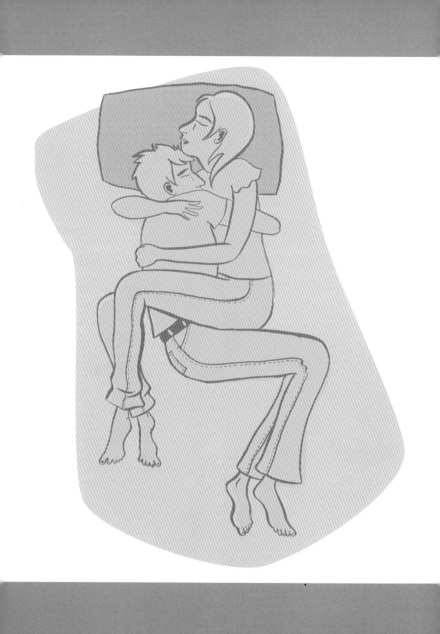

MAIN SQUEEZE

This is the ultimate I-can't-get-enough-of-you embrace. If you find yourself speaking baby-talk to each other, you need The Main Squeeze. Both of you are lying on your sides face to face. She wraps her legs around his waist, and embraces his head with her lower arm. He will have the impulse to wrap both of his arms around her body, but it is best only to wrap his upper arm around her. Keep the lower arm snuggled in tight between the two bodies, otherwise his arm will quickly lose all feeling under the weight of her body (even if she is light as a feather, as of course she is.).

MELTING BUTTER

On those nights when one of you is just too dang tired to do a thing, here is a simple and smooth way to melt into each other. She lies flat on her back, legs straight, and arms out to the side. He lies on his side resting his head on her shoulder and clutches her with both arms and legs. For an added dash of sizzle try this variation: he pulls his legs up and rests them between her torso and his so that he is almost rolled into a ball alongside her. Either version makes for a perfect sleep-through-the-night cuddle

TUG O' LOVE

Does your partner's tossing and turning keeping you up all night? Here is your chance to tie her down, but nicely. You both lie side-by-side on your backs with your arms and legs slightly spread apart. Hook your arms at the elbow and interlace your legs. Hold on tight, it could be a bumpy ride!

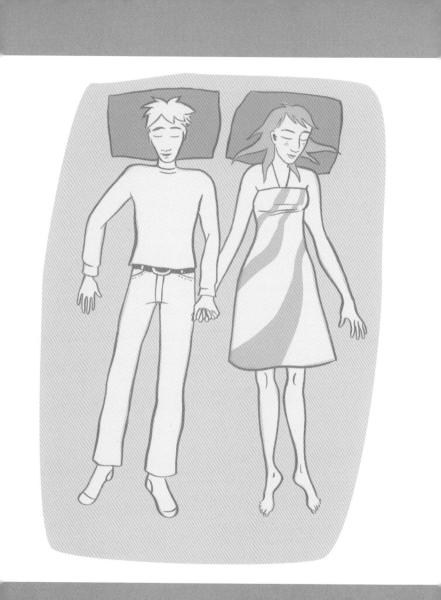

CHERRY POPSICLES

It is a hot and sticky summer night, the **AC** is on the fritz, and there is just no way are you going to let anyone cuddle up beside you. Fear not—there is an incredibly simple cuddle that is as refreshing as a cherry popsicle that leaves your tongue an unnaturally deep shade of red. Both of you lie on your backs in your own space on the bed and just reach your hand out to the side and grab hold. It is an endearingly simple act that says, "even in the worst of situations, I am here for you."

THE X FACTOR

This is the perfect middle of the night cuddle. Maybe you've had a bad dream, your mind won't seem to slow down, or you just feel like you need a small reminder that you are not alone. There's no need to wake your partner up to make contact. Just lay your leg over his. It's intimate, it's connected, and it is surprisingly reassuring. Be careful not to rest your leg directly on top of his knee, or he may wonder why he is limping in the morning. Okay, now you can get back to sleep.

BREAKFAST IN BED

This tasty cuddle is about as simple and intimate as it gets. She lies on her back and he lies face down directly on top of her like two pancakes, resting his head on her chest. Don't be afraid to rest all your weight on each other. That bond is one of the great pleasures of this position. If there is a big difference in weight, you will both be more comfortable with the lighter person on top. Once in place, there are any number of options and variations to this position. Both of your arms are free to gently run your hands through each other's hair, lightly stroke each other's faces, arms, and back. This closeness also encourages intimate conversation and whispered sweet nothings. Your legs can either be in a straight and flat position, or he can bend his knees, straddling her in a frog legs position. Mmmm, pancakes with frogs legs. Now there's a dish you never thought you would want to whip up!

9:30 P.M.

Any time is the right time for cuddling, and this position practically makes time stand still. Think of your bodies as the hands of a clock. She is lying on her back with her legs pointing to the six. He is lying on his stomach with his head on her chest and his face turned to the side toward her face. He is lying at a ninety-degree angle from her, so his legs are pointing to the nine. Both of their arms are loosely wrapped around the other's upper body. This is such a close and comfortable position for both that you are likely to find yourselves drawn into quiet conversation; eventually your breathing may start to match, and before you know it you will both start to drift off to sleep at your new bedtime, 9:30 P.M.

SPOONING

One of the basic utensils in the cuddling drawer, this position has been a popular one since cuddling began. It is simple, comfortable, and it gives you a warm, deep down two-bugs-in-a-rug type of feeling. You both lie on your sides facing in the same direction so that your bodies are aligned. This is most easily achieved when the taller partner is in back. The back person hugs the front person with their hands meeting at the front person's chest. With bent hips and knees, your bodies conform to one another, fitting perfectly together.

FORKING

This twist on the spooning position is all about full-frontal hugging. Again, lie on your sides, but this time face to face, and embrace each other with a bear-hug-strength hug. Just like Spooning, your legs are bent at the hips and knees, but now they are threaded through each other like the tines of two forks facing each other. This is a cuddle of enthusiasm and is not meant to last hours, but you can easily transition from this position into many other long lasting cuddles, including the always comforting Come to Papa.

THROUGH THE WOODS

This position may have you feeling like your body is the road winding "over the river and through the woods . . ." She lies on her back with her knees bent, her feet on the bed, and one arm out to the side for him to snuggle into. He lies on his side with his head resting on her shoulder and his top arm gently resting on her upper body. He slides his legs through the tunnel formed by her bent legs and bends his as well. This is particularly restful and calming (just like grandma's house should be).

TWO PILLOWS

There is nothing quite as soothing as the gentle rise and fall of your partner's breath. She lies on her side in a comfortable curled-up position using his stomach as her pillow. He lies on his back with his head on a regular pillow and runs his fingers through her hair and over her back. The soothing touch and calming rhythm combine to ease her into her dreams.

THE HUSBAND

Not surprisingly, my wife came up with this one. Why buy one of those husband pillows to prop yourself up in bed with when you've got the real thing right there? He lies on his side with his legs bent at the hips and the knees. His head is resting on his bottom arm and a pillow, and his upper arm is resting comfortably in front of him. She fits perfectly sitting between his arm and legs, using his body as her support. He is free to fall asleep while she watches TV, reads a book, or works on her laptop.

CHEEK TO CHEEK

Sometimes it is hard to decide who gets to lay your head down and who gets to be the comforting shoulder, so why don't you both do both at the same time? You lie head to head in a straight line so that the tops of your heads can rest on each other's shoulders. Experiment with the position of your arms. You may find that extending the arm of the shoulder your partner's head is resting on may make for a more comfortable pillow. Unless you have an unusually long bed (or you are both particularly short) you will need to lie with bent knees for you to both easily fit on a bed.

CHAPTER 2

Couch Canoodling: Snuggling on the Sofa

SURF & SNUGGLE

It doesn't get any simpler (or better!) than this. He sits on one end of the couch with a pillow in his lap. She lies on her side or her back and rests her head on the pillow. This position gives him the freedom to put his feet up, grab a drink, channel surf, or even read a book—just make sure you have everything you need within reach, because once she falls asleep you'll be stuck there.

SARDINES

Being crammed together like sardines in a can has never felt so good. You both lie on your backs at opposite ends of the couch so that your legs run the full length of your partner's body and your feet fit snugly in your partner's underarms. Depending on your heights and the length of your couch, you may need to sit up a bit to make this work perfectly for you. You can relax in this cozy position for hours, and it is ideal for intimate conversations, naps, and reading.

THE TIMES TOGETHER

He wants the comics and she wants the travel section—don't let the mound of papers get in the way of a Sunday cuddle. Each of you grabs a section and lies at opposite ends of the couch, resting your heads on an armrest or pillow. Your legs should slide through the other's legs with both of his on the outside of hers. Both of your legs are bent with the feet resting on either side of your partner's hips or stomach. And, whenever you want to share a particularly interesting tidbit, just move your knees to either side for a clear view of your partner.

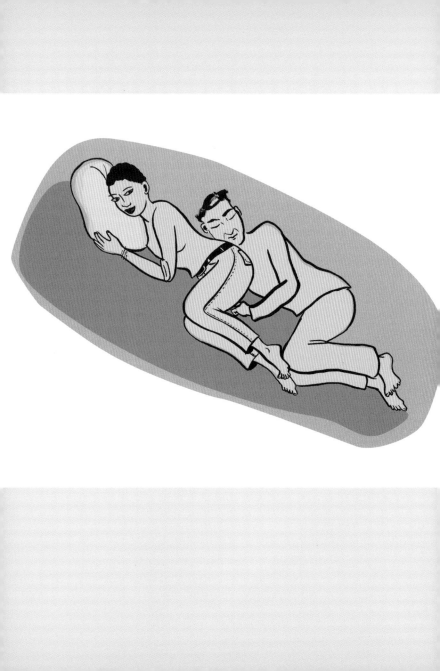

TWO PEAS IN A POD

They say imitation is the sincerest form of flattery. Well, this position is the perfect compliment for both of you. She lies on her side with her head resting on the armrest. Her legs are bent at the hips and at the knees, but her knees should only be bent enough to keep her legs on the front of the cushion. He lies in exactly the same position, except he uses her hips as his pillow. This is great for watching TV, napping, or just lazing about.

TICKLISH DELIGHT

Lie on your sides at opposite ends of the couch, resting your heads on the armrests or pillows. Weave your legs through each others so that your inner thighs are resting on each other. This is a particularly easy and cozy way to while away the hours on the couch with each other. And, if you want to drive your partner crazy, you are perfectly positioned to tickle his feet . . . but then so is he.

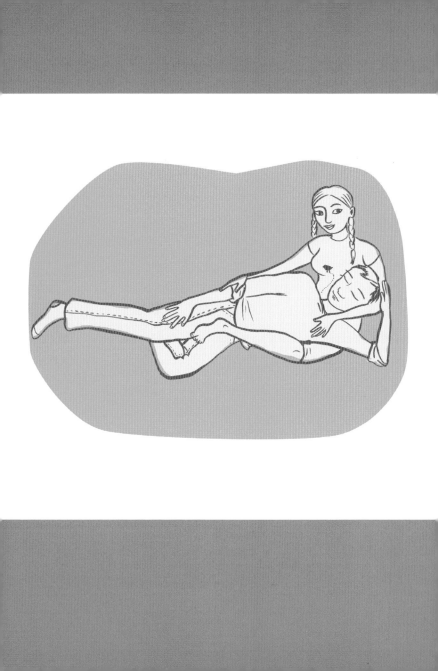

HORIZONTAL HOLD

This is one of the most affectionate and endearing cuddles you can perform on a couch. She sits at the end of the couch with her upper body leaning sideways on the armrest and her legs running the length of the couch. Her top leg remains straight along the back of the cushion and her bottom leg bends so that her knee touches the front edge of the cushion. He lies on his side with his torso fitting in the space between her legs and his head cradled in her arms. This is an easy position for both of you to hold for hours of caressing, soothing conversation, or a DVD double feature.

SPLISH SPLASH

No need for twists, flips, and half-gainers to make a big splash with this cozy position. To dive into this cuddle, you both lie on your sides in the exact same position facing each other with your arms around each other's upper bodies. The position of your legs is just the way they would be if you were taking your last big step before you dive off a diving board. Your bottom leg is perfectly straight and your upper leg is bent at the knee with the foot even with your other leg's calf. Your bent legs are intermingled, with her leg lying on top of his, making for some very welcome intimate contact. This is an easy position to maintain for long stretches of time, and is perfect for some quiet pillow talk and long luxurious afternoon naps. Degree of difficulty: 0.0

THE LAYER CAKE

This position looks as sweet as it sounds, and the icing on the cuddle is how good it feels. You both sit on the couch next to each other and stack your legs one on top of the other in layers (his, hers, his, hers). You both reach your arms around each other and lean into each other to fully engulf one another. This is a passionate cuddle, but not one you will want to hold for too long or you will soon find your legs falling asleep.

THE MOST COMFY CHAIR

This may remind you a bit of sitting on Santa's lap when you were a child, but even as an adult this remains a particularly tender way to tell each other what you want for Christmas and every day of the year: each other. He sits on the couch and she sits sideways on his lap. He reaches his arms around her waist giving her support and she leans her upper body against his. She has her hands free to massage his neck and head. Now that's a perfect gift.

LEAN TWO

This perennial favorite is one of the most utilized positions in the entire cuddle catalogue because of its simplicity, comfort, and the ease with which it allows you both to tangle over the clicker. He leans over and rests his head on the armrest of the couch or against his bent arm (depending on the height of the armrest). His legs are bent comfortably at the hip and knees, resting his feet against her thighs. She is leaning over in the exact same position, leaning against his arm and holding his hands on his legs. He may be tempted to reach his arm around her neck to cradle her head, but this will put her head in an awkward position. Simply leaning on him will leave you both comfortable enough to stay in one position for hours of viewing—though deciding whose show to watch may not be quite as easy.

THE MATCHING PILLOW SET

Sure, the couch has plenty of cushions, and there may even be a bunch of throw pillows strewn about, but it is still pretty hard to find a more comfortable place to lay your head than on some well-padded part of your partner. You can both make a pillow out of your partner by lying on your sides, heads pointed in opposite directions. Your feet are pointing toward the armrests and your torsos are criss-crossing in the center of the couch. Your legs are bent at the hips and the knees. He lies behind her using the slope of her hips as a pillow, and she lies her head on his thighs.

Tête à Tête

Whether it is marveling at the beauty of her eyes or just pointing out the sprouting zits, sometimes there is no greater pleasure then tuning out the rest of the world and giving each other a little face time. Sitting face-to-face, he places his legs on either side of her, and she bends her legs and rests them in the space between their bodies. Wrap your arms around each other and stare into each other's eyes lovingly. When that starts to feel a bit cheesy, you are also in the perfect position for a killer staring contest.

PART 2

Public Displays of Affection

CHAPTER 3

Walking With My Baby: Hand Holds and Embraces

THE OLD-FASHIONED

This is how you picture your grandparents walking down the street in olden days, but it is a simple and profound way to express your connection to your partner in any era. Link your arms with the forearms resting on one another. Your free arms can swing or rest on the hand of the linking arm. Best for slow walks through the park, leisurely strolls along the countryside, and walking your daughter down the aisle. Not recommended for bustling city streets.

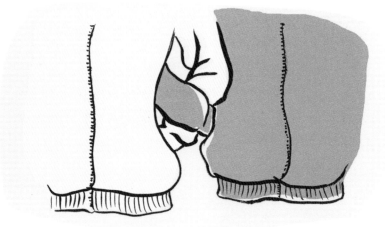

THE NEW-FASHIONED

A more casual take on The Old-Fashioned; again, arms are linked at the forearms, but one partner's hand makes its way into a pant or jacket pocket and the other person's arm rests on top of it. All the connection with none of the effort. Not recommended for walking your daughter down the aisle.

On chilly days, try this variation: the Cold-Fashioned. Simply link your arms at the elbows, but this time both of you slip your hands into your coat pockets. All the connection, all the warmth.

THE YAWN MANEUVER

Back when you were thirteen years old you had to summon the courage of a thousand men to try out "the move." Well, whether or not it paid off then, I can guarantee it'll do the job now. So, sit right next to each other, put your arm around her shoulder, and snuggle up close.

PUBLIC DISPLAYS OF AHHHH!

Find a wall and lean against it. You are now perfectly poised for the smoochiest ahhh-filled PDA out there. Resting all of your weight against the wall, bend one leg and rest your foot against the wall. Your knee is now sticking out in front of you and making an inviting seat for her to climb on. The two of you are standing face to face, clutching, hugging, kissing, and stroking each other with your weight comfortably leaning into the wall. Be warned though, use of this cuddle in public may induce nausea in unattached passersby.

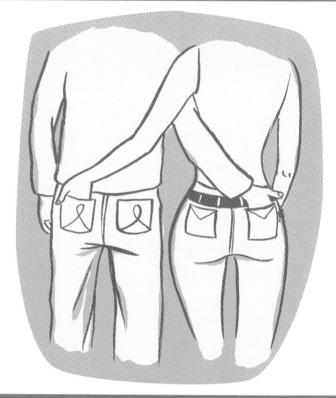

THE PICK POCKET

You probably don't want to use this on your first date, but once you have both reached the "I-just-can't-keep-my-hands-off-your-butt" stage, it is time for The Pick Pocket. Walking side by side, slip your inside hands down into your partner's back pocket, resting your thumb outside the pocket. And if you are lucky, there is always that added bonus—spare change!

YOUR HONEY OR YOUR LIFE

Don't worry, this hold may look a little like a stick-up, but there is nothing illegal about it. She stands in back and slightly to the side of him, and wraps one arm around the tops of his shoulders (not too tightly, you don't want to choke him!) and takes hold of his other hand at his side. He stands there and feels the love. Don't be surprised if this catches the attention of some local law officer, but only because he wishes he had it so good.

PARTNERS IN TIME

This hold not only shows that you love who you are with, but that you even like each other. This has a real buddy feel to it. Walking side by side, one of you puts your arm around the other's waist or can slip your hand into their back pocket, while they put their arm over your shoulder so that their arm is hanging down over your chest.

THE POSE

So, you are walking along side by side, just quietly minding your own business, when suddenly you are overtaken by an irresistible wave of rapturous, gooey love for one another. You are ready for the Pose. You reach your arms around each other's waists. Pull each other in tightly, turn your heads in the same direction, and squeeze your cheeks together as if someone were about to snap your picture. This feels so silly and fun that you can't help but smile a big old cheek-to-cheek grin. You can keep walking in this position, though you probably won't win any races.

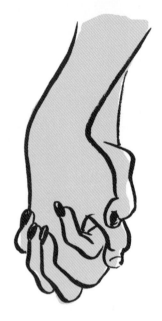

THE WEAVE

The classic romantic handhold. One of the most universally recognized hand-holds, the weave is particularly powerful for amorous pairings. Perhaps it is because the fingers of both hands are completely interwoven, forming a strong and intimate bond—a connection that is both a public and private manifestation of how closely joined together you two have become.

THE VELCRO TOUCH

Whether you are leading your partner through the rough terrain of crowded city streets or trying to hold on to each other against an onslaught of oncoming department store clearance sale shoppers, you need The Velcro Touch. Hold your fingers and thumb together tightly and curve your fingers so that they form a hook. Link both of your hooks together and grip tightly. No one can break this apart, not even a blue-light special.

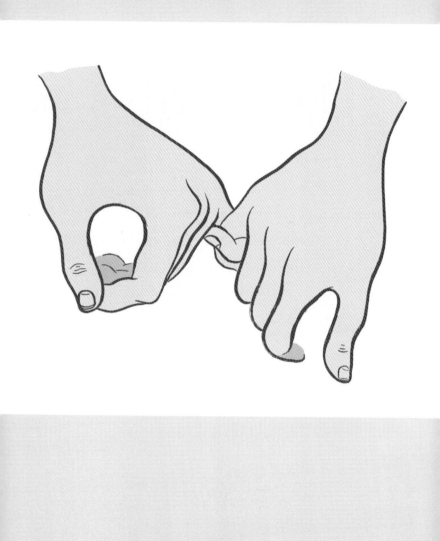

PINKY PLAY

Sometimes less is more. There is a certain confidence and maturity that comes with this hold; it is a simple and unadorned way to feel a connection with your partner. Interlock your pinkies and continue walking with the certainty that right here and right now you are with the right person. You can pinky-bet it will feel good.

CROSS MY HEART

If you find your relationship turning into a bit of a wrestling match, the Cross My Heart clasp just might settle the score. Walking side by side, join your same-sided arms (right and right or left and left) and bend them at the elbow. Link hands at the thumbs and wrap the rest of your fingers around the outside of your partner's hand. She can reach around and hold her other hand around his waist while the linked hands are held close to her chest. Maintain a firm grip, but try not to actually arm wrestle.

TEAM PLAYERS

This hold is a little like having a set of shoulder pads, but while these may not protect you from an oncoming linebacker on Super Bowl Sunday, they certainly will help you withstand feeling down in the dumps on any given day. This has a real I'm-your-partner-and-we-can-face-anything-together feel to it. Walking next to each other, he slips his arm under hers and rests his hand on the shoulder nearest him, and she rests her hand on his shoulder. Now you can recover from any fumble.

ARM IN ARM

This is the classic arm-around-your-honey way to walk down the block. Walking side by side, She wraps her arm around his waist, and he wraps his arm around her shoulder. If there is a large difference in heights, it will generally be easier for the taller person to put their arm around their partner's shoulder. However you divide up the roles, you should make sure you are comfortable. You will use this walk often and throughout the entire span of your relationship.

THE HUGGLE

A hug is a hug, right? No, a simple hug is the most basic of embraces: a routine and momentary maneuver employed for greetings, good-byes, and other everyday interactions with family and friends. But a Huggle is a whole different level of embrace. It is reserved only for those dearest to our hearts. It is a tender move that demands more than a passing moment and communicates more than a passing affection for someone. Think of it as more of a standing snuggle than a cursory salutation. Both of you wrap your arms completely around each other, pressing your bodies fully and willfully into each other. You can rest your heads on each other's shoulder and gently rub each other's back. Give in to the instinct to close your eyes and, most importantly, linger in the warmth of each other's embrace.

THE PICK-ME-UP

This truly is the universal cure for anyone feeling a little sad or gloomy. He wraps his arms around her upper body, giving her a bear hug, and then leans back, lifting her off the ground. She holds on for dear life, clutching him with both of her arms around his neck. This move is most effective when performed as a surprise and should last only a few seconds (for the sake of his lower back). This is sure to bring a smile to both of your faces.

THE GLEAP

There are few more boisterously joyful ways to share your affection for one another than with this embrace. When you find yourselves running wildly toward each other, at an airport arrivals terminal, for instance, this is the cuddle of choice for you. With a running start, she leaps with glee into his waiting arms, wrapping her legs tightly around his waist. She locks herself in place by linking her ankles together, and he secures her by hugging his arms around her upper back. Hold tightly and promise never to be apart again.

THE THRESH HOLD

Don't get nervous, now. Whether this relationship is headed down the aisle or not, it always feels good to sweep someone off their feet. He lifts her into his arms, holding her under her knees and around her back. She rests her arms around his neck, and you both stare lovingly into each other's eyes. It's also the perfect way to chivalrously carry her over puddles.

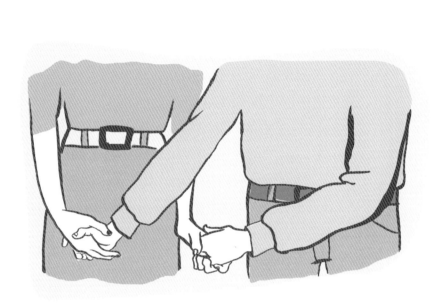

PROMENADE

This figure-skating-like hold says, "I love you so much that I am willing to look a little goofy in public." Walking side by side, his shoulder is ever-so-slightly in front of hers. You link like-sided hands (right hand to right hand or left hand to left hand) with his arm completely crossing in front of her body to hold her hand, which is resting straight at her side. With her other hand, she can place her arm around his shoulder or repeat the same position with the other hand for the full figure-skater effect and get ready to Double Lutz with the best of them.

THE DIP

On the dance floor or off, nothing says "I trust you" more than The Dip. He prepares for the move with her standing sideways, perpendicular to him. He places his arms around her shoulders and her waist and she wraps her arm closest to his around his waist and the other hand holds onto his shoulder. To go into The Dip, he steps one leg out to the side and supports her torso as she bends backward. She continues to hold onto his waist and shoulder as she leans, slightly bending her standing leg while kicking her other leg off the floor as far as possible. (For extra style points, her feet should be pointed.) Here is the trick to a successful dip: She never gives her weight fully over to him. She maintains control and balance with her standing leg. She is always in control of how far back she bends. While in the dip, always maintain eye contact. Stay in the dip for just a moment or two and then come back to a standing position. For even more style points, perform the move with a rose in your mouth.

ABOUT THE AUTHOR

Rob Grader is a writer, actor, television producer, massage therapist, and committed cuddling devotee. He is the author of the award-winning book *The Cheap Bastard's Guide to New York City* (Globe Pequot Press) and he created and produced the A&E reality series *House of Dreams*. As an actor, Rob has appeared in *American Splendor*, *Law & Order*, *Law & Order: SVU*, and *The Job*, as well as on the stages of regional theaters around the country. As a licensed massage therapist for over ten years, he has relieved many an aching back working at many of the leading spas in Manhattan. He lives in New York City where he cuddles the days away with his wife, Karen and their newborn son, Roscoe.

ABOUT THE ILLUSTRATOR

Leela Corman is an illustrator, cartoonist, painter, and bellydancer. She lives in Brooklyn.